The Shadow Work Journal

A Guided Journey Through the Unconscious Self

Flavio Pires Molina

For permission requests, write to the publisher at:

flavio.pires.molina@gmail.com

First Edition – Dec/2025

Cover design: Monika Swatek

Interior design: Flavio Pires Molina

ISBN: 9781919449401

For my first teachers, my parents,
Neylor and Maria Lucia.

For my amazing wife, Monika.

And for my greatest inspiration, my sons,
Mateus and Gabriel.

Contents

FOREWORD

In the year of C. G. Jung's sesquicentennial, whose work continues to inspire growing academic interest and foster the most diverse individuations, it seems I was the one who received a gift. Dr. Molina's invitation to write the preface for this book was a pleasant surprise and a great honor. However, I must secretly confess to readers that such an invitation also came laden with enormous apprehension: how could I write brief, objective lines worthy of a work that received such dedication from its author? I thought about retreating in the face of such responsibility, would I be up to the challenge? What should I do? Write or embarrass myself? Since the ego seemed to offer me nothing, I thought it better to search in the shadow and see what happened. The result? Well, you're already reading the result!

That being so, in general terms, I feel one can say that the shadow is representative of those psychic aspects not known or not accepted by the ego; it constitutes its opposite side, and it is something also linked to individuality. It can be very useful if well worked and integrated into consciousness, but should this not occur and it becomes hostile, such a need for integration will be more urgent, and seeking understanding about it will, in turn, be inevitable. One must not forget that it can also be seen as a significant social function by allowing us inclusion in the collective, for there is where we are merely human among humans, our qualities and excellences elevate us above all that.

The work of integration, most commonly developed in psychotherapy, would then occur through the recognition of what one denies is present within one's own psyche but can be easily projected onto another, especially if this other is of the same sex as the one projecting. Such recognition of the shadow, under psychotherapy, can also arise from dream interpretation; in these, it may appear personified by dream characters who present themselves as being of the same sex as the dreamer.

One can therefore observe that the shadow contains those aspects that probably should no longer be repressed but rather integrated into consciousness. In such a task, the ego must humbly submit itself to a sacrifice, risking dealing with everything that initially seems negative, shameful, or repugnant but which may, ultimately, not be so. It is not easy because, in general, the individual's tendency is always to consider only what seems socially agreeable.

As a clinical psychologist who works with psychotherapy, I am fully aware that there is no infallible technique for all cases; the integration of the shadow is always something specific, individual—the maxim "each case is a case" must always be taken into account. The shadow exists; it exerts its influence on the individual psyche, and in this way, a long process of work to integrate it may be necessary.

In our current world, where the shadowy aspect of the human being seems increasingly present, where both collectively and individually we can be increasingly psychically contaminated, the dangers are many—and it is at this point that the work developed by Dr. Molina in the following pages may prove to be a valuable contribution.

Geraldo Fortes Bustamante Neto, psychologist, PhD

PREFACE

This journal was born from necessity, my own.

For years, I maintained what appeared to be a perfectly ordered life: military service as a Lieutenant Dentist in the Brazilian Air Force, advanced degrees, academic positions, clinical practice. I had mastered the art of discipline, precision, and professional composure. But beneath this carefully constructed exterior, questions persisted: *Who am I beneath these roles? What have I abandoned to get here? What does it mean to be truly whole?*

Shadow work gave me answers, but not the comfortable kind. It showed me that the same discipline that made me an effective officer and competent scientist had also taught me to exile essential parts of myself. Wholeness, I discovered, doesn't come from perfection but from integration, from finally turning toward everything I'd spent decades avoiding.

The irony wasn't lost on me: I was trained in the medical model, identify the problem, eliminate it, cure the patient. Shadow work required the opposite: recognize what's been rejected, approach it with curiosity, integrate rather than eliminate. This went against everything my training had taught me.

Yet it was precisely this journey, from the structured world of military service and scientific research to the mysterious realm of the unconscious, that showed me what true strength looks like. Not the strength to maintain a flawless exterior, but the courage to face what lies beneath it.

I created *The Shadow Work Journal* as the companion I wished I'd had: structured enough to guide you through unfamiliar territory, spacious enough to hold whatever emerges, and compassionate enough to remind you that this difficult work is also sacred work.

Dr. Bustamante's foreword beautifully articulates the theoretical foundation of shadow work. What follows in these pages is the practical application, 83 prompts across 12 chapters, each designed to help you recognize, understand, and integrate your shadow.

This is not easy work. There will be moments when you want to close this journal and return to the comfortable illusion of the persona. I encourage you to stay. The parts of yourself waiting in the darkness are not your enemies, they are the keys to your wholeness.

This is not about becoming "better." It's about becoming whole.

Welcome to your journey.

Flavio Pires Molina, PhD.
Dublin, Ireland
2025

INTRODUCTION: MEETING YOUR SHADOW

"The shadow is not a problem to be solved, but a truth to be integrated."
Carl Jung

What lies beneath the surface of who you think you are?

What parts of yourself have you disowned, hidden, or buried in the depths of your unconscious?

The shadow, Jung's term for the repressed, denied, and rejected aspects of the self, holds the key to wholeness.

What Is the Shadow?

The concept of the shadow comes from the work of Carl Gustav Jung, the Swiss psychiatrist and founder of analytical psychology. Jung observed that every human psyche contains both light and dark aspects: parts that are conscious and accepted, and parts that are hidden from awareness.

He described the shadow as the unconscious side of the personality, everything we deny, repress, or fail to recognize in ourselves. These are not only the traits we consider "negative", such as anger, envy, selfishness, or desire, but also the qualities we fear to own: power, brilliance, creativity, and passion.

Jung wrote, "Everyone carries a shadow, and the less it is embodied in the individual's conscious life, the blacker and denser it is." Yet he also reminded us that "the shadow is ninety percent pure gold."

The shadow, therefore, is not simply darkness; it is the unlived life within us. By acknowledging it, we reclaim energy, authenticity, and lost vitality. By refusing it, we project it onto others and live half a life.

Why Shadow Work Matters

To do shadow work is to turn toward what we've spent our lives avoiding. It is the process of making the unconscious conscious, of meeting the parts of ourselves we've exiled with curiosity, honesty, and compassion.

This is not about becoming "better" or "more spiritual." It's about becoming whole. Shadow work invites you to embrace the full range of your humanity: the sacred and the messy, the loving and the fearful, the light and the dark.

When you meet your shadow, you meet yourself.

How to Use This Journal

- Be honest. Your shadow thrives in secrecy and shame. Honesty is the antidote.
- Take your time. This is not a race. Some prompts may take days or weeks to answer fully.
- Return often. Shadow work is cyclical. You may discover new layers each time you revisit a prompt.
- Hold yourself with compassion. You are uncovering material that was hidden for a reason. Be gentle.

Let us begin.

1
THE MASK WE WEAR

The Persona Archetype

The persona is the mask we show the world...but beneath every mask lies the face we're afraid to show.

1.1 What is the Persona?

The persona is the mask we wear in our daily interactions with the world. Carl Jung described it as the social face we present to others, the roles we play at work, with family, and in our communities. It's how we want to be seen, rather than who we truly are beneath the surface.

Think of your persona as a necessary adaptation to social expectations. When you're professional at work, friendly with neighbors, or responsible with family, you're using different aspects of your persona. These aren't fake versions of you; they're real, but they're not the whole story.

1.2 Why the Persona Matters on Your Journey

As you move toward wholeness and the Self, understanding your persona is crucial. Many people make the mistake of either:

- Over-identifying with their persona (believing they are only the role they play)
- Rejecting their persona entirely (thinking it's "fake" and must be destroyed)

Both extremes block your growth. The persona serves an important function; it helps you navigate society and connect with others. The key is recognizing it's a tool, not your true identity.

1.3 Signs Your Persona May Be Too Rigid

- You feel exhausted from "keeping up appearances"
- You can't remember what you genuinely enjoy versus what you think you should enjoy

- You feel empty or hollow despite external success
- You're terrified of being seen without your social mask
- You've lost touch with your authentic feelings and desires

PROMPT 1:
Describe the version of yourself you present to the world. What qualities do you emphasize? What do you want others to believe about you?

PROMPT 2:
What parts of yourself do you hide in social situations? What would people be surprised to learn about you?

PROMPT 3:
When do you feel most "fake" or inauthentic? What situations force you to wear the thickest mask?

PROMPT 4:

Who in your life has seen you without your mask? How did it feel to be truly seen?

PROMPT 5:

What would you lose if you dropped your persona entirely? What are you protecting by keeping it in place?

PROMPT 6:

Write a letter from your authentic self to your persona. What does your true self want your mask to know?

REFLECTION: The persona is necessary; it helps us navigate social reality. But over-identification with the mask leads to emptiness. Notice where you can be more authentic without endangering yourself.

1.4 Working with Your Persona

The goal isn't to destroy your persona, but to develop a conscious relationship with it. Ask yourself:

1.5 Reflection Questions:

- What roles do I play in my daily life? (professional, parent, friend, partner)
- Which parts of these roles feel authentic? Which feel forced?
- What would I lose if I couldn't play these roles anymore?
- Who am I when no one is watching?
- What parts of myself do I hide to maintain my social image?

1.6 The Path Forward

As you journey toward the Self, you'll learn to hold your persona lightly, using it when helpful, but not clinging to it as your identity. You'll discover there's much more to you than any single role or image. The authentic Self emerges when you can honor your social responsibilities while remaining connected to your deeper truth.

Remember: The persona is like clothing. You need it to move through the world, but you are not your clothes. The work is learning to dress appropriately for each situation while knowing the person underneath remains whole and real.

As you move through this journal, notice when you're wearing your persona and when you're touching something deeper. Both are valid; both are part of your journey to wholeness.

2
THE DISOWNED SELF

Projection and Recognition

We don't see the shadow directly. Instead, we project it onto others. The people who trigger us most intensely are mirrors, reflecting back the parts of ourselves we refuse to acknowledge.

2.1 What is Projection?

Projection is the psychological process of seeing parts of yourself in others, especially the parts you've rejected, denied, or never recognized. Carl Jung understood that we unconsciously place our own unacknowledged qualities, feelings, and traits onto other people, then react to them "out there" rather than recognizing them within ourselves.

When you strongly dislike someone for being "arrogant" or "weak," or when you're inexplicably drawn to someone's "confidence" or "freedom," you may be encountering disowned parts of yourself. These people become mirrors, reflecting back what you cannot or will not see in your own psyche.

2.2 Why We Project

Projection is not a character flaw; it's a natural psychological mechanism. We project because:

- Certain traits threaten our self-image (the persona you explored in Chapter 1)
- We learned early that some qualities were unacceptable (too aggressive, too sensitive, too ambitious, too needy)
- Our psyche seeks wholeness by showing us what we've split off

The irony is that projection keeps us fragmented. By placing parts of ourselves "out there," we remain incomplete within.

2.3 Signs You May Be Projecting

- You have intense emotional reactions to certain people (hatred, envy, idealization)

- You repeatedly encounter the "same type" of difficult person
- You're convinced everyone else has a quality you lack
- You can't understand why "those people" behave that way
- You feel morally superior or inferior to specific groups
- You're fascinated or repulsed by traits you claim not to possess

2.4 The Shadow Connection

Projection is intimately tied to what Jung called the Shadow, the rejected, denied, or unknown aspects of ourselves. Your Shadow contains:

- Qualities you were taught were "bad" (anger, selfishness, sexuality, aggression)
- Positive traits you never claimed (creativity, power, beauty, intelligence)
- Undeveloped potential you've ignored

When you project your Shadow, you give away your own power and possibility. You see villains and heroes everywhere except in the mirror.

PROMPT 7:
Who irritates you most in your life right now? List their most annoying qualities in detail.

PROMPT 8:
Looking at the list above, which of these qualities do you possess but refuse to admit? Be ruthlessly honest.

PROMPT 9:

Think of someone you intensely dislike or judge. How are you similar to this person in ways you don't want to acknowledge?

PROMPT 10:

What qualities do you pride yourself on NOT having? (Example: "I'm not selfish," "I'm not weak," "I'm not manipulative.")

PROMPT 11:

Can you find moments in your life when you've exhibited the exact qualities you pride yourself on not having? Describe them.

PROMPT 12:
What would it mean about you if you admitted to having the qualities you judge in others?

PROMPT 13:
Who do you admire or idealize? What qualities do they have that you deny in yourself?

REFLECTION: Jung said, "Everything that irritates us about others can lead us to an understanding of ourselves." Your triggers are your teachers.

2.5 Working with Projection

The path to wholeness requires reclaiming your projections, recognizing that what you see "out there" often points to something "in here." This doesn't mean everyone is just a mirror; it means your strong reactions are valuable information.

2.6 Reflection Questions:

- Who in my life triggers intense negative emotions? What specific traits bother me most?
- Who do I idealize or envy? What qualities do they have that I tell myself I lack?
- What do I repeatedly criticize in others? Could I possess any version of this trait?
- What would happen if I owned this quality as part of myself?
- What parts of myself did I have to disown to be accepted by my family, culture, or community?

2.7 The Path Forward

Withdrawing projections is humbling work. It means admitting that the "enemy" or "hero" out there is also within you. But this is where freedom lives. When you reclaim your projections:

- You stop giving your power away
- You see others more clearly, as they truly are
- You access rejected strengths and gifts
- You move closer to the authentic Self

Remember: Projection isn't something to feel ashamed about; it's a signpost. Every projection is an invitation to become more whole. When you catch yourself in a strong judgment or idealization, pause and ask: "What is this showing me about myself?"

As you move through this chapter, pay attention to your reactions to others. They are offering you golden keys to unlock disowned parts of yourself. This is the work of integration: gathering all the scattered pieces of who you are.

3
SHAME AND THE HIDDEN WOUNDS

The Inner Critic

Shame is the guardian of the shadow. It keeps our disowned parts locked away in darkness, whispering that we're too broken, too flawed, too much, or not enough.

3.1 What is Shame?

Shame is the deeply painful feeling that something is fundamentally wrong with who you are not what you did, but who you are at your core. Unlike guilt, which says "I made a mistake," shame whispers "I am a mistake." In Jungian terms, shame forms around the wounds we carry in our psyche, the places where you learned you were unacceptable, unlovable, or inherently flawed.

These hidden wounds often develop early in life, when we're most vulnerable. A critical parent, a traumatic experience, rejection by peers, or simply absorbing the unspoken messages of our culture can create deep shame that shapes how we see ourselves for decades.

3.2 Why Shame Matters on Your Journey

Shame is one of the greatest barriers to wholeness. It keeps parts of yourself locked away in darkness, deemed too terrible to acknowledge or integrate. Remember the persona from Chapter 1? Shame often determines which mask you wear, constructed specifically to hide what you believe is shameful beneath.

And the projections from Chapter 2? They frequently originate in shame. You reject in others what you've been taught to reject in yourself. Shame creates the splits in your psyche that prevent you from becoming whole.

Jung understood that you cannot become the Self while leaving wounded, shame-bound parts of yourself in exile. Integration requires bringing compassion to your hidden wounds.

3.3 Signs You're Carrying Hidden Shame

- You avoid certain topics or memories at all costs
- You feel a visceral sense of being "defective" or "damaged"
- You experience intense fear of being truly seen or known
- You engage in perfectionism or overachievement to compensate
- You have a harsh, critical inner voice that attacks you
- You sabotage success or intimacy when things get too good
- You feel undeserving of love, belonging, or happiness
- Certain emotions (anger, need, desire) feel dangerous or forbidden

3.4 The Origins of Shame

Shame doesn't arise in isolation. It develops through:

- Childhood experiences: Criticism, neglect, abuse, or conditional love
- Cultural messages: About your body, gender, sexuality, race, or class
- Traumatic events: That convinced you something is wrong with you
- Family systems: Where certain feelings or truths couldn't be spoken
- Internalized voices: Of those who couldn't accept parts of you

These wounds live in your psyche as what Jung might call "complexes": charged emotional clusters that get triggered, taking you over in moments of vulnerability.

PROMPT 14:
What are you most ashamed of about yourself? What would devastate you if others knew?

____
____
____
____
____
____
____
____

PROMPT 15:

When did you first feel this shame? Can you remember a specific moment or period in your life?

PROMPT 16:

What does your inner critic say to you most often? Write down its exact words.

PROMPT 17:

Whose voice is your inner critic using?(a parent? Teacher? Bully? Religious figure?)

PROMPT 18:

What would happen if you stopped believing your inner critic? What are you afraid would happen?

PROMPT 19:

Write a compassionate response to your inner critic. What would a loving friend say to those harsh words?

PROMPT 20:

What parts of yourself have you deemed "unacceptable?" Why are they unacceptable?

REFLECTION: Shame thrives in silence. The act of naming what you're ashamed of begins to dissolve its power. You are not your worst moment. You are not your harshest thought.

3.5 Working with Shame and Hidden Wounds

Healing shame requires moving toward what you've spent a lifetime moving away from. This is tender, courageous work that cannot be rushed. The goal is not to eliminate shame overnight, but to develop a different relationship with your wounded places.

3.6 Reflection Questions:

- What parts of myself do I feel are fundamentally unacceptable or wrong?
- When did I first learn to feel ashamed of this part of me? Who taught me this?
- What do I fear would happen if others saw this aspect of me?
- How has shame shaped the persona I present to the world?
- What would self-compassion sound like toward my wounded parts?
- If my shame could speak, what would it be trying to protect me from?

3.7 The Path Forward

Shame loses its power when it's brought into the light with compassion. This doesn't mean sharing your wounds with everyone; it means first acknowledging them to yourself without judgment. As you witness your own pain with tenderness rather than criticism, something shifts.

You begin to see that your wounds are not evidence of your defectiveness; they're evidence of your humanity. Everyone carries hidden wounds. The difference is whether you let them remain in shadow, controlling you from the darkness, or whether you bring them into consciousness where healing becomes possible.

Remember: Your shame points to the most vulnerable, often youngest parts of yourself, the parts that needed protection and got rejection instead. These parts are still waiting for you to come back for them with love. This is not weakness; this is the hero's journey inward.

As you move through this chapter, approach yourself with the gentleness you would offer a frightened child. Your hidden wounds don't make you broken; they make you human. Integration means welcoming all of yourself home, especially the parts you were taught to abandon.

4
ANGER AND THE FORBIDDEN RAGE

The Destroyer Archetype

Many of us were taught that anger is dangerous, ugly, or inappropriate. So we suppress it, and it becomes part of our shadow. But anger contains vital energy and important information about our boundaries and values.

4.1 What is Forbidden Rage?

Anger is a natural, vital emotion that signals when your boundaries have been violated, your needs ignored, or your dignity compromised. Yet for many people, anger has become forbidden, pushed into the Shadow and deemed too dangerous, destructive, or unacceptable to feel or express. This forbidden rage doesn't disappear; it goes underground, shaping your life from the darkness.

In Jungian psychology, repressed anger becomes part of the Shadow, that collection of qualities you've disowned. When anger is forbidden, it leaks out in passive-aggression, chronic resentment, depression, physical illness, or sudden explosive outbursts that seem to come from nowhere. The rage you won't acknowledge consciously doesn't vanish; it controls you unconsciously.

4.2 Why Anger Matters on Your Journey

Wholeness requires reclaiming all of your emotions, including anger. Remember the shame from Chapter 3? Anger is often one of those hidden wounds; you may have learned that your anger made you bad, dangerous, or unlovable. So you created a persona (Chapter 1) that's always nice, accommodating, or calm, while projecting your anger onto others (Chapter 2), seeing them as the aggressive or unreasonable ones.

4.3 Why Anger Carries Essential Information. It tells you:

- Where your boundaries need strengthening
- When you're being treated unjustly

- What matters deeply to you
- Where you've betrayed yourself to keep peace

Without access to your anger, you cannot fully protect yourself, advocate for your needs, or honor your truth. You remain fragmented, giving away your power to avoid feeling a "forbidden" emotion.

4.4 Signs You've Disowned Your Anger

- You pride yourself on "never getting angry" or always staying calm
- You feel depressed, numb, or exhausted without knowing why
- You have passive-aggressive tendencies or make cutting remarks
- You fantasize about telling people off but never do
- You're terrified of conflict or others' anger
- You develop physical symptoms (headaches, stomach issues, tension)
- You have sudden rage explosions that shock even you
- You feel guilty or ashamed when you do express anger
- You're drawn to angry people or find yourself in explosive relationships

4.5 The Origins of Forbidden Rage

You weren't born afraid of your anger. You learned to fear it through:

- Childhood conditioning: "Good girls/boys don't get angry," anger was punished or ignored
- Dangerous anger models: A parent's rage was frightening or destructive
- Cultural messages: About who's allowed to be angry (often shaped by gender, race, or class)
- Traumatic experiences: Where your anger made things worse or couldn't protect you
- Survival adaptations: Suppressing anger was necessary to stay safe or loved

Over time, you internalized the belief that your anger itself is the problem, rather than recognizing it as valuable information about your inner and outer world.

PROMPT 21:

What were you taught about anger growing up? Was it allowed in your family? How was it expressed or suppressed?

PROMPT 22:

What are you angry about right now but haven't allowed yourself to fully feel or express?

PROMPT 23:

Who do you need to be angry at but have been too afraid, guilty, or "nice" to confront?

PROMPT 24:

Write an unsent letter of rage to someone who has hurt you. Hold nothing back.

PROMPT 25:

What boundaries have been crossed in your life that you didn't defend? Why didn't you defend them?

PROMPT 26:

If you fully owned your anger, what would change in your life? What would you say or do differently?

PROMPT 27:
What healthy forms of anger expression are available to you?(Movement, art, advocacy, boundary-setting?)

REFLECTION: Anger is not the enemy. Unacknowledged anger that leaks out as passive aggression, resentment, or self-sabotage is the real danger. Your anger is trying to tell you something. Listen.

4.6 Working with Anger and Forbidden Rage

Reclaiming your anger doesn't mean becoming aggressive, cruel, or out of control. It means developing a conscious relationship with this energy. Healthy anger is:

- Informative: It tells you what matters and where boundaries are needed
- Protective: It mobilizes you to defend yourself and others'
- Energizing: It provides fuel for necessary change
- Time-limited: When expressed appropriately, it moves through and releases

4.7 Reflection Questions:

- What messages did I receive about anger growing up? Who was allowed to be angry in my family?
- What do I fear would happen if I fully felt and expressed my anger?
- Where in my life do I feel resentful, frustrated, or chronically annoyed?
- What boundaries have I failed to set because I'm afraid of seeming "angry" or "difficult?"

- How does my body hold suppressed anger? (tension, pain, illness)
- If my forbidden rage could speak, what would it say? What does it want me to know?

4.8 The Path Forward

Integration means bringing your anger out of the Shadow and into consciousness. This is gradual work; you don't go from complete suppression to healthy expression overnight. Start by simply noticing when anger arises, without immediately pushing it away or acting it out.

Learn to distinguish between destructive rage (which harms) and healthy anger (which protects and informs). Your anger is not your enemy; the unconscious expression of it is. When you reclaim this powerful emotion, you reclaim a vital part of your life force.

Remember: Your anger is not evidence of your badness; it's evidence of your aliveness. It shows you care, that you have limits, that you matter. Wholeness includes the full spectrum of human emotion. You don't have to be perpetually peaceful to be spiritual or good. You have to be real.

As you move through this chapter, give yourself permission to feel what has been forbidden. Your anger has been waiting in the darkness for your acknowledgment. When you finally turn toward it with curiosity instead of fear, it can transform from a destructive force into a powerful ally on your journey to wholeness.

5
THE DARK DESIRES

Sexuality, Power, and the Taboo

The shadow contains not only what we consider "bad" but also what we consider forbidden, dangerous, or socially unacceptable, including our desires for power, pleasure, and freedom.

5.1 What are Dark Desires?

Dark desires are the wants, longings, and appetites you've labeled as wrong, shameful, or dangerous, the ones you barely admit to yourself. These aren't necessarily destructive or immoral desires; they're simply the ones that don't fit the image you've constructed of who you "should" be. In Jungian terms, these desires live in the Shadow, exiled because they threaten your persona or contradict the values you were taught to uphold.

Dark desires might include: wanting power or recognition, craving luxury or pleasure, longing for freedom from responsibility, desiring sexual experiences outside convention, wanting to be seen as desirable, needing to rest or be selfish, or even the desire to abandon everything and start over. What makes them "dark" is not their inherent nature, but your relationship with them, the fear, shame, and denial surrounding them.

5.2 Why Dark Desires Matter on Your Journey

You cannot become whole while disowning your desires. When you reject what you want, you fragment yourself, creating the very splits you've been exploring: the acceptable persona (Chapter 1) that hides forbidden wants, the projection (Chapter 2) of seeing your desires in others, the shame (Chapter 3) of being a person who wants "wrong" things, and the anger (Chapter 4) that builds from chronic self-denial.

Your desires, even the uncomfortable ones, carry vital information about who you are and what you need. They're not commands to act on every impulse, but invitations to understand yourself more deeply.

Denying them doesn't make you more evolved; it makes you more fragmented.

Jung understood that integrating the Shadow means acknowledging all of yourself, including the parts that want things your conscious mind finds unacceptable. This is where true transformation happens.

5.3 Signs You're Suppressing Dark Desires

- You feel numb, disconnected from wanting anything at all
- You judge others harshly for pursuing pleasure, ambition, or freedom
- You have secret fantasies you'd never admit to anyone
- You feel intensely envious of people living more freely
- You're drawn to stories, films, or people who embody what you've forbidden yourself
- You experience sudden compulsive behaviors or "acting out"
- You feel like you're living someone else's life or following a script
- You pride yourself on being "above" certain needs or wants
- You feel resentful about sacrifices you've made but can't articulate why

5.4 The Origins of Forbidden Desires

Your desires became dark through:

- Religious or moral conditioning: Certain wants were sinful, selfish, or spiritually inferior
- Family values: What you wanted contradicted what your family deemed acceptable
- Gender expectations: Your desires didn't match cultural norms for your gender
- Survival needs: Wanting things felt dangerous or threatened your belonging
- Traumatic associations: Certain desires became linked with pain, punishment, or loss
- Perfectionism: The belief that "good" people don't want certain things

Over time, you learned to split off these desires, creating an acceptable self that wants only "right" things, while the rest of your longing went underground.

PROMPT 28:
What desires do you judge yourself for having? What do you want but feel you "shouldn't" want?

PROMPT 29:
What fantasies do you keep secret, even from yourself? What scenarios play in your mind that you push away?

PROMPT 30:
Where in your life do you crave power or control but pretend you don't?

PROMPT 31:
What would you do if you had no fear of judgment or consequences? How would you live differently?

PROMPT 32:
What aspects of your sexuality have you repressed or denied? What judgments do you hold about your sexual self?

PROMPT 33:
If your desires are not harming others, why do you believe they're wrong? Whose voice is that?

PROMPT 34:
What would it feel like to accept your desires without acting on the destructive ones? Can you hold complexity?

____
____
____
____
____
____
____
____

REFLECTION: Desire itself is not dangerous. Repressed desire that controls you from the unconscious is dangerous. Integration means acknowledging what's true without being ruled by it.

5.5 Working with Dark Desires

The goal isn't to act on every desire without discernment. It's to acknowledge what you want without immediate judgment or repression. Desires become dangerous when they're unconscious and denied; that's when they control you through compulsion, projection, or sudden eruptions.

5.6 When You Bring Desires Into Consciousness, You Can:

- Understand what they're really telling you about your needs
- Choose consciously whether and how to respond to them
- Distinguish between destructive impulses and legitimate longings
- Find healthy ways to honor what you truly need

5.7 Reflection Questions:

- What do I want that I've never allowed myself to admit?
- What desires do I judge most harshly in others? Could these be my own disowned wants?
- If I had permission to want anything without judgment, what would it be?

- What was I taught about desire? Which desires were acceptable, and which were forbidden?
- How do I punish myself for wanting? (through guilt, self-denial, sabotage)
- What would change in my life if I honored my authentic desires?

5.8 The Path Forward

Reclaiming your dark desires doesn't mean abandoning your values or acting impulsively. It means developing an honest relationship with your whole self, the part that strives for goodness and the part that wants pleasure, power, rest, recognition, freedom, or passion.

Wholeness includes desire. You are allowed to want. You are allowed to pursue what brings you alive, even if it looks different from what you thought you "should" want. The Self emerges not from perfection but from integration, accepting all of who you are, including the wanting, hungry, ambitious, pleasure-seeking parts.

Remember: Your desires are not evidence of your corruption, they're evidence of your humanity and vitality. What you've called "dark" may simply be what's been kept in the dark. When you shine light on your authentic longings with compassion and discernment, you reclaim the energy you've spent suppressing yourself. This is not indulgence; this is becoming whole.

As you move through this chapter, practice honoring your truth: you are a person who wants things. This doesn't make you selfish or base, it makes you alive. The journey to the Self requires knowing and accepting what you desire, then choosing consciously how to live with that knowledge.

6
ENVY, GREED, AND THE HUNGRY GHOST

The Insatiable Self

We live in a culture that both glorifies and shames ambition, success, and wanting more. In the shadow lurks our envy, our greed, our sense of scarcity and never-enough-ness.

6.1 What are Envy and Greed?

Envy is the painful feeling that arises when someone else has what you want, coupled with the wish that they didn't have it. Greed is the insatiable hunger for more, more possessions, attention, success, or love, driven by a sense of inner emptiness that never feels filled. In Jungian psychology, these emotions often live in the Shadow because they contradict the generous, content persona most people want to project.

Envy whispers "they don't deserve what they have; I do." Greed says "I need more to be enough." Both are considered shameful emotions in most cultures, yet both are deeply human responses to feelings of lack, inadequacy, or wounded self-worth. What makes them problematic isn't their existence, but what happens when they remain unconscious and denied.

6.2 Why Envy and Greed Matter on Your Journey

When you cannot acknowledge your envy or greed, these feelings don't disappear, they distort your relationships and self-perception. You might find yourself sabotaging others' success, feeling chronically dissatisfied despite abundance, or unable to celebrate anyone's good fortune. The dark desires from Chapter 5 often manifest as envy when you see others living the life you've forbidden yourself.

Envy and greed are actually pointing to something deeper: unmet needs, disowned ambitions, or core beliefs about scarcity and unworthiness. The shame (Chapter 3) around these feelings keeps them in darkness, while your persona (Chapter 1) works overtime to appear grateful and satisfied. Meanwhile, you project (Chapter 2) your envy onto others, seeing them as greedy or attention-seeking.

Wholeness requires acknowledging these uncomfortable truths: sometimes you want what others have, and sometimes you want more than you have. This doesn't make you a bad person; it makes you human.

6.3 Signs You're Suppressing Envy or Greed

- You feel bitter or resentful when good things happen to others'
- You can't genuinely celebrate friends' successes or happiness
- You minimize others' achievements or find flaws in their good fortune
- You feel a chronic sense of "not enough" no matter what you have
- You hoard resources, attention, or opportunities
- You compete constantly, even when unnecessary
- You feel entitled to what others have earned
- You experience shame after wanting more or feeling envious
- You judge "greedy" or "jealous" people with particular harshness

6.4 The Origins of Envy and Greed

These feelings develop from:

- Early deprivation: Not having enough materially or emotionally as a child
- Comparison wounds: Being unfavorably compared to siblings or peers
- Conditional worth: Learning your value depends on having or achieving more
- Scarcity mindset: Believing there's not enough (love, success, recognition) for everyone
- Unmet needs: Childhood needs for attention, validation, or security that were never satisfied
- Cultural messages: That your worth is measured by what you have or achieve

When these wounds remain unhealed, envy and greed become unconscious attempts to fill a void that can never be filled from the outside.

PROMPT 35:
Who are you envious of? What do they have that you want? Be specific and honest.

PROMPT 36:
What does your envy reveal about your own disowned dreams and desires?

PROMPT 37:
Where in your life do you feel a sense of scarcity? Not enough time, money, love, recognition, success?

PROMPT 38:
What are you greedy for? What do you want more of, even when you have enough?

PROMPT 39:
What would "enough" look like to you? Can you even imagine feeling satisfied?

PROMPT 40:
How does comparison steal your peace? When do you measure yourself against others?

PROMPT 41:
What would you do differently if you believed there was enough for everyone, including you?

____

____

____

____

____

____

____

____

REFLECTION: Envy shows us what we haven't given ourselves permission to pursue. Greed points to an inner emptiness seeking external fulfillment. The question isn't "How do I get more?" but "What am I truly hungry for?"

6.5 Working with Envy and Greed

The key is understanding what these feelings are really about. Envy often reveals:

- Disowned desires and ambitions
- Areas where you've given up on yourself
- Qualities you haven't developed in yourself
- Beliefs that you're not allowed to have what you want

6.6 What Greed often reveals

- Deep feelings of inner emptiness or unworthiness
- Unmet childhood needs still crying out for satisfaction
- Fear that you'll never have enough to feel safe or valuable
- Confusion between what you actually need and symbolic substitutes

6.7 Reflection Questions:

- Who do I envy? What specifically do they have that I want?
- What does my envy reveal about my disowned desires or abandoned dreams?

- When do I feel the insatiable hunger of greed? What am I really hungry for?
- What did I not get enough of as a child? (attention, love, security, recognition)
- How do I try to fill my inner emptiness? Does it work?
- What would "enough" actually feel like? What would I need to believe about myself to feel it?

6.8 The Path Forward

Transforming envy and greed begins with honest acknowledgment without shame. When you feel envy, instead of suppressing it or acting it out, ask: "What is this showing me about what I want or need?" When you feel greed's insatiable hunger, ask: "What am I really starving for?"

Often, what you're truly seeking isn't the external thing itself but internal qualities: worthiness, security, significance, or love. No amount of external acquisition can fill an internal void. The work is turning inward to address the original wounds and beliefs driving these feelings.

As you do this, envy can transform into inspiration, "if they can have it, perhaps I can too." Greed can transform into healthy ambition and clear knowledge of what you genuinely need versus what you're using to fill emptiness.

Remember: Envy and greed are not moral failings, they're messengers from your wounded self, showing you where you feel lacking, where you've abandoned your own desires, or where childhood needs remain unmet. When you listen with compassion instead of shame, these difficult feelings can guide you toward healing and wholeness.

As you move through this chapter, practice radical honesty about these forbidden feelings. Your envy shows you what you want. Your greed shows you what you're missing. Both are invitations to come home to yourself and heal the wounds that created the sense of lack in the first place.

7
THE VICTIM AND THE TYRANT

Power Dynamics in the Shadow

Within each of us lives both a victim and a perpetrator, a tyrant and a martyr. These polarities exist in the shadow, alternating their grip on our psyche depending on the situation.

7.1 What are Victim and Tyrant Dynamics?

The Victim and Tyrant are archetypal patterns that represent two sides of the same psychological dynamic, the abuse of power. The Victim experiences life from a position of powerlessness, constantly at the mercy of circumstances or others. The Tyrant wields power destructively, controlling or dominating to avoid vulnerability. In Jungian psychology, these are Shadow patterns that most people carry in some form, often unconsciously.

You may identify primarily with one role while projecting the other onto people around you. But here's the truth: both exist within your psyche. The Victim and Tyrant are not separate people but two responses to feeling unsafe, wounded, or out of control. They are survival strategies that once protected you but now keep you trapped.

7.2 Why These Dynamics Matter on Your Journey

These patterns connect deeply to everything you've explored. Your persona (Chapter 1) may be built around being the "good victim" who never asserts power, or the "strong one" who never shows vulnerability. You project (Chapter 2) the opposite role onto others, seeing tyrants everywhere when you identify as victim, or seeing weakness in others when you identify with dominance. Shame (Chapter 3) often fuels both patterns, and the anger (Chapter 4) you've disowned either collapses into victim helplessness or explodes into tyrannical control.

Neither role allows for authentic selfhood. The Victim gives away all power; the Tyrant hoards it defensively. Wholeness requires transcending both, reclaiming your agency without dominating others.

7.3 Signs You're Caught in Victim Dynamics

- You feel perpetually at the mercy of circumstances or others' choices
- You frequently feel helpless, trapped, or without options
- You attract relationships where you're mistreated or overlooked
- You wait for others to rescue you or change so your life can improve
- You feel resentful but powerless to set boundaries or leave
- You tell your story of suffering repeatedly, defining yourself by what happened to you
- You resist taking responsibility for your choices or their consequences
- You feel morally superior through your suffering

7.4 Signs You're Caught in Tyrant Dynamics

- You need to control situations, people, or outcomes to feel safe
- You become aggressive, domineering, or intimidating when threatened
- You struggle to tolerate others' autonomy or differences
- You use guilt, manipulation, or force to get your way
- You see vulnerability as weakness and must always appear strong
- You rationalize cruel behavior as "necessary" or "for their own good"
- You feel powerful only when others are diminished or submissive
- You fear being controlled, so you control first

7.5 The Origins of Victim and Tyrant Patterns

These dynamics form through:

- Early powerlessness: Childhood experiences of being controlled, abused, or helpless
- Identification with the aggressor: Becoming like those who hurt you to feel safe
- Learned helplessness: Repeated experiences where your actions didn't matter
- Family systems: Witnessing or experiencing these patterns as "normal"
- Trauma responses: Fight (tyrant) or freeze/fawn (victim) becoming habitual
- Cultural conditioning: Messages about power, gender, and worthiness

Both patterns are attempts to manage fear and vulnerability, but neither leads to authentic power or genuine safety.

PROMPT 42:
Where in your life do you play the victim? In what situations do you feel powerless and blame others?

PROMPT 43:
What does your victim identity protect you from? What responsibilities can you avoid by staying powerless?

PROMPT 44:
Where have you been a perpetrator? When have you harmed, manipulated, or used power over others?

PROMPT 45:
What did you gain from these actions? What need were you trying to meet through controlling or harming others?

PROMPT 46:
Can you hold both truths: that you have been victimized and that you have victimized others? How does it feel?

PROMPT 47:
Where do you need to reclaim your power? Where do you need to relinquish inappropriate power?

PROMPT 48:
What would authentic empowerment look like for you, not power over others, but power with yourself?

____

____

____

____

____

____

____

____

REFLECTION: The victim and tyrant are two sides of the same coin. Both are attempts to manage powerlessness. True power comes from taking responsibility for your choices while acknowledging the real constraints and harms you've faced.

7.6 Working with Victim and Tyrant Dynamics

Integration means recognizing both patterns within yourself. You're not only the victim of your past, you also have agency now. And you're not only powerful through dominance, you have strength in vulnerability too. True power is neither dominance nor submission; it's the capacity to be authentic, set boundaries, and allow others their autonomy.

7.7 Reflection Questions:

- In what areas of my life do I feel powerless? Where do I refuse to take responsibility?
- Where do I try to control others or outcomes? What am I afraid will happen if I don't?
- Who in my past embodied these patterns? Which did I vow never to become?
- How do I use my suffering to avoid action or change?
- When do I intimidate, manipulate, or dominate others? What vulnerability am I protecting?
- What would it mean to have power without controlling others?

- What would it mean to acknowledge my wounds without identifying as a victim?

7.8 The Path Forward

Transcending victim and tyrant dynamics requires developing what Jung called the mature ego, one that can hold both strength and vulnerability, power and humility, autonomy and connection. This means:

- Acknowledging past hurt without being defined by it
- Reclaiming agency over your choices now
- Setting boundaries without dominating
- Showing vulnerability without collapsing into helplessness
- Taking responsibility without shame

You move beyond these patterns when you realize: you are not powerless, and you don't need to control others to be safe. Authentic power comes from knowing yourself, honoring your truth, and allowing others theirs.

Remember: The victim and tyrant within you are wounded parts trying to protect you. They're not your enemies, they're strategies that once helped you survive. But wholeness requires evolving beyond survival into authentic living. You have more options now than you did when these patterns formed. You can be powerful without dominating. You can be vulnerable without being helpless. This is integration.

As you move through this chapter, observe when you slip into victim or tyrant patterns. Both are invitations to reclaim authentic power, the kind that comes from self-knowledge, not from domination or submission. True strength includes tenderness. True vulnerability includes agency.

8
THE UNLOVED CHILD

Childhood Wounds and Core Beliefs

Our shadow is largely formed in childhood, when parts of us were deemed unacceptable by caregivers, society, or circumstances. The unloved child still lives within, carrying beliefs formed in those early years.

8.1 What is the Unloved Child?

The Unloved Child is the wounded, younger part of your psyche that carries the pain of not receiving the love, attention, acceptance, or protection you needed. This isn't necessarily about dramatic abuse or abandonment, it's about any significant gap between what your developing self needed and what you received. In Jungian terms, this is often called the "wounded child" or "inner child," a complex that holds unprocessed pain, unmet needs, and core beliefs formed when you were most vulnerable.

This child lives within you still, influencing your relationships, self-worth, and capacity for joy. The Unloved Child believes: "I am not enough," "I am too much," "Love is conditional," "I must earn belonging," or "I am fundamentally unlovable." These beliefs were formed in childhood but continue to operate in your adult life, often unconsciously.

8.2 Why the Unloved Child Matters on Your Journey

This wounded part is at the heart of almost everything you've explored. The persona (Chapter 1) was often constructed to protect the Unloved Child, becoming who you thought you needed to be to finally earn love. Your projections (Chapter 2) frequently originate here, you see rejection or judgment in others because the Unloved Child expects it. The shame (Chapter 3), forbidden anger (Chapter 4), dark desires (Chapter 5), and envy (Chapter 6) all connect to these early wounds of not being loved as you were.

Until you turn toward this wounded part with compassion, it remains frozen in the past, running your present life from the shadows. Wholeness requires meeting the Unloved Child and offering what was never given.

8.3 Signs You're Carrying an Unloved Child

- You feel fundamentally unworthy of love or belonging
- You overwork, overachieve, or over-give to earn approval
- You can't tolerate being alone with yourself
- You stay in relationships where you're mistreated because it feels familiar
- You experience abandonment panic when people pull away slightly
- You struggle to believe compliments or love, certain they're mistaken
- You feel like an imposter, always about to be exposed as inadequate
- You recreate childhood dynamics in adult relationships
- You have difficulty setting boundaries or saying no

8.4 The Origins of the Unloved Child

This wound forms through:

- Emotional unavailability: Parents present physically but absent emotionally
- Conditional love: Affection tied to behavior, achievement, or compliance
- Neglect or abuse: Direct experiences of being unwanted, criticized, or harmed
- Parentification: Having to care for parents' needs instead of your own
- Impossible standards: Never being good enough, smart enough, or lovable enough
- Generational trauma: Parents unable to give what they never received
- Simple misattunement: Even well-meaning parents missing crucial emotional needs

The child you were internalized these experiences as proof of your inadequacy, not recognizing that the failure was in what you received, not in who you were.

PROMPT 49:
What did you need as a child that you didn't receive? Love, safety, validation, attention, freedom?

PROMPT 50:
What messages did you receive about who you were allowed to be? What parts of you were celebrated? Punished?

PROMPT 51:
What did you have to do to earn love and approval? What strategy did you develop to survive emotionally?

PROMPT 52:
Write a letter to your childhood self. What does that child need to hear from you now?

PROMPT 53:
What core beliefs do you hold about yourself? (Example: "I'm not enough," "I'm too much," "I'm unlovable," "I must be perfect.")

PROMPT 54:
How have these core beliefs shaped your adult life? Where do you see them playing out in your relationships, work, and choices?

PROMPT 55:
What would your life look like if you didn't believe these things about yourself?

____

____

____

____

____

____

____

____

REFLECTION: The child you were still lives within you, carrying old wounds and outdated survival strategies. Shadow work is, in part, re-parenting this inner child, giving them what they needed then and deserve now.

8.5 Working with the Unloved Child

Healing this wound requires becoming the loving adult to the child you were. This isn't about blaming your parents or dwelling in victimhood, it's about acknowledging the truth of what happened and taking responsibility for your healing now. The Unloved Child is still waiting for someone to turn toward them with love, and that someone is you.

8.6 What This inner child needs

- To be seen and acknowledged
- To have their feelings validated
- To be told it wasn't their fault
- To receive the love, protection, and acceptance they were denied
- To grieve what they didn't receive
- To be released from the burden of earning love

8.7 Reflection Questions:

- What did I most need as a child that I didn't receive?
- What did the child I was conclude about themselves based on how they were treated?

- When do I still operate from these childhood beliefs today?
- What does my inner child need to hear from me now?
- How do I abandon myself the way I was once abandoned?
- If I could go back and speak to the child I was, what would I say?
- What would it mean to give myself now what I needed then?

8.8 The Path Forward

Integrating the Unloved Child means developing a compassionate internal relationship with this wounded part. You become the parent you needed, offering patience, acceptance, and unconditional love to the parts of yourself that never received it. This is not self-indulgence; it's essential healing work.

As you turn toward this child with love rather than shame or rejection, something profound shifts. You begin to separate your worth from what you received. You recognize that you were always lovable, the failure was never yours. You can grieve what you didn't get without being destroyed by it. You can offer yourself now what no one else can give you: complete self-acceptance.

Remember: The Unloved Child within you is not broken or damaged beyond repair. They are simply waiting to be met with the love they always deserved but never received. You are not too much or not enough, you never were. What happened to you was not evidence of your unlovability; it was evidence of others' limitations. The journey to wholeness includes gathering this precious, wounded child into your arms and finally bringing them home.

As you move through this chapter, speak to the child you were with the tenderness you would offer any hurt child. They have been carrying this pain alone for so long. Your love now, for yourself, for the child you were, is the medicine that heals the deepest wounds and makes integration possible.

9
THE FEMININE AND MASCULINE SHADOWS

Anima and Animus

Jung spoke of the anima (the feminine in men) and animus (the masculine in women), but these archetypal energies exist in everyone, regardless of gender. When rejected, they become shadow.

9.1 What are Feminine and Masculine Shadows?

In Jungian psychology, the anima (the feminine principle in those with masculine consciousness) and animus (the masculine principle in those with feminine consciousness) represent the contrasexual aspects of the psyche. But beyond these internal figures, we all carry cultural and personal shadows around femininity and masculinity, the rejected, denied, or distorted aspects of these archetypal energies within ourselves.

These are not about biological sex or gender identity, but about psychological principles: the feminine (receptive, intuitive, nurturing, emotional, cyclical, relational) and the masculine (active, rational, protective, goal-oriented, linear, autonomous). Both energies exist in everyone, regardless of gender, but culture, family, and personal history determine which aspects you've developed and which you've disowned.

9.2 Why These Shadows Matter on Your Journey

Your persona (Chapter 1) was likely constructed around culturally approved expressions of gender. You've projected (Chapter 2) your disowned feminine or masculine qualities onto others. You carry shame (Chapter 3) around traits deemed inappropriate for your gender. Your forbidden anger (Chapter 4) or desires (Chapter 5) may be forbidden precisely because they're "too masculine" or "too feminine." And the Unloved Child (Chapter 8) often learned that certain aspects of themselves were unacceptable based on gender expectations.

Wholeness requires integrating both principles within yourself, not conforming to stereotypes, but reclaiming the fullness of human capacity regardless of what culture said was appropriate for "people like you."

9.3 Signs You've Disowned Feminine Energy

- You're always doing, achieving, or pushing forward without rest
- You dismiss emotions as weakness or irrationality
- You struggle with receptivity, intuition, or allowing things to unfold
- You devalue care work, nurturing, or relationships as "less important"
- You're uncomfortable with softness, vulnerability, or asking for help
- You view sensitivity or emotional expression as shameful
- You have difficulty being rather than doing
- You're cut off from your body, cycles, or natural rhythms

9.4 Signs You've Disowned Masculine Energy

- You struggle to assert yourself, set boundaries, or take decisive action
- You wait for others to make things happen rather than initiating
- You feel guilty about ambition, power, or pursuing your goals
- You abandon yourself to keep peace or please others'
- You can't access healthy aggression or protective anger
- You feel paralyzed in the receptive mode, unable to move forward
- You dismiss logic, structure, or planning as "too rigid"
- You're uncomfortable with your own authority or leadership capacity

9.5 The Origins of Gendered Shadows

These shadows form through:

- Cultural conditioning: Rigid gender roles that split human qualities into acceptable/unacceptable
- Family modeling: Parents who embodied or rejected certain energies
- Trauma around gender: Being punished, shamed, or violated for being "too masculine" or "too feminine"
- Systemic inequality: Social structures that devalue feminine or distort masculine principles

- Survival adaptations: Suppressing certain qualities to stay safe or accepted
- Internalized oppression: Carrying society's prejudices within your own psyche

Over generations, these splits have wounded both men and women, forcing everyone into rigid boxes that deny psychological wholeness.

PROMPT 56:
What qualities do you consider "feminine?" Which of these do you embrace? Which do you reject or judge?

____
____
____
____
____
____
____
____

PROMPT 57:
What qualities do you consider "masculine?" Which of these do you embrace? Which do you reject or judge?

____
____
____
____
____
____
____
____

PROMPT 58:
How were you taught to be(or not be) based on your gender? What was forbidden to you?

____
____

PROMPT 59:
What aspects of emotional expression feel dangerous or shameful to you? Vulnerability? Aggression? Softness? Strength?

PROMPT 60:
Where in your life would benefit from more receptivity, intuition, or nurturing energy?

PROMPT 61:
Where in your life would benefit from more assertion, logic, or protective energy?

PROMPT 62:
What would it feel like to embrace the full spectrum of human qualities, beyond gendered conditioning?

REFLECTION: Wholeness requires integrating all aspects of human experience, the soft and the strong, the receptive and the assertive, the feeling and the thinking. Gender conditioning creates artificial splits. Healing requires transcending these binaries.

9.6 Working with Feminine and Masculine Shadows

Integration means reclaiming the fullness of both energies within yourself. This isn't about performing gender differently; it's about accessing the complete range of human capacities. You need both receptivity and assertion, both feeling and thinking, both nurturing and protecting, both intuition and logic.

Ask yourself: Which energy am I most comfortable with? Which feels foreign or dangerous? The one you've rejected holds the key to your next level of wholeness.

9.7 Reflection Questions:

- What did I learn about femininity and masculinity growing up? Which was valued, which was denigrated?

- Which aspects of feminine energy (receptivity, emotion, intuition, nurturing) have I rejected in myself?
- Which aspects of masculine energy (assertion, logic, autonomy, ambition) have I rejected in myself?
- Who in my life embodies the qualities I've disowned? What do I judge in them?
- How was I punished or shamed for being "too much" or "not enough" in terms of gender?
- What would it mean to honor both feminine and masculine within myself?

9.8 The Path Forward

Wholeness transcends the binary. It means developing your capacity for both action and receptivity, both strength and tenderness, both independence and connection. You're not trying to become "balanced" in some artificial way, but rather to access whatever energy is needed in each moment, without shame or limitation.

The feminine doesn't belong only to women; the masculine doesn't belong only to men. These are human capacities, archetypal energies that everyone carries. When you reclaim your disowned energy, you become more fully yourself, not more stereotypically gendered, but more complete.

Remember: You contain multitudes. The parts of yourself that don't fit narrow gender expectations aren't mistakes or flaws, they're essential aspects of your wholeness. Healing means embracing the full spectrum of who you are: soft and strong, receptive and active, emotional and rational, nurturing and ambitious. You don't have to choose. Integration means saying yes to all of it.

As you move through this chapter, notice which energy feels most foreign or uncomfortable. That's where your growth lies. The journey to wholeness requires reclaiming both feminine and masculine principles within yourself, not as concepts but as lived capacities. You are more than any gender role could ever contain.

10
THE GOLDEN SHADOW

Reclaiming Your Light

Not everything in the shadow is dark. We also repress our power, creativity, brilliance, and beauty. The golden shadow contains the positive qualities we've disowned because they felt too big, too much, or too dangerous.

10.1 What is the Golden Shadow?

Most people think of the Shadow as purely dark, the rejected, shameful parts you hide. But Jung recognized that the Shadow also contains gold: the positive qualities, strengths, gifts, and potential you've denied or never claimed. The Golden Shadow consists of your disowned light, beauty, power, intelligence, creativity, wisdom, charisma, or talent that you've projected onto others while insisting you yourself could never possess such qualities.

This is perhaps the most tragic form of self-denial: not rejecting your darkness, but rejecting your brilliance. The Golden Shadow keeps you small, diminished, and living far below your potential. You admire these qualities in others, envy them (Chapter 6), or idealize those who embody them, never recognizing that you're seeing a reflection of your own unlived life.

10.2 Why the Golden Shadow Matters on Your Journey

Throughout this journey, you've been reclaiming rejected parts: the persona's mask (Chapter 1), your projections (Chapter 2), your shame and wounds (Chapter 3), forbidden emotions like anger (Chapter 4), hidden desires (Chapter 5), envy (Chapter 6), power dynamics (Chapter 7), and the unloved child (Chapter 8). But the path to wholeness isn't complete until you reclaim your gold.

Your gifts and potential often threaten your persona as much as your flaws do. The Unloved Child learned that being too bright, too talented, or too powerful was dangerous, it invited envy, punishment, or abandonment. So you dimmed your light to stay safe, to belong, to not threaten others. But you cannot become the Self while disowning your magnificence.

10.3 Signs You're Rejecting Your Golden Shadow

- You genuinely cannot see your own gifts, talents, or positive qualities
- You deflect compliments or feel embarrassed by praise
- You attribute your successes to luck, others' help, or external factors
- You experience intense admiration or envy toward people with qualities you claim not to have
- You feel like an imposter when you succeed
- You sabotage yourself when you're on the verge of fully showing up
- You make yourself smaller to avoid outshining others'
- You're waiting for permission or validation to claim your power
- You believe others are special but you are fundamentally ordinary

10.4 The Origins of the Golden Shadow

You learned to reject your light through:

- Tall poppy syndrome: Being cut down when you stood out or excelled
- Family dynamics: Threatening a parent's ego or sibling's position by being "too much"
- Cultural messages: About who gets to be powerful, beautiful, intelligent, or successful
- Traumatic success: Being punished, envied, or abandoned when you shone
- Modesty as virtue: Learning that claiming your gifts is arrogance or pride
- Scarcity belief: The idea that your success diminishes others or threatens belonging
- Unworthiness wound: The core belief from the Unloved Child that you don't deserve good things

You internalized the message: it's safer to be small, ordinary, and unremarkable than to claim your full power and potential.

PROMPT 63:
What talents or gifts do you downplay or hide? Why do you make yourself smaller?

PROMPT 64:
When have you been told you're "too much?" Too loud, too intense, too smart, too sensitive, too ambitious?

PROMPT 65:
What would people say about you if you showed up fully? What are you afraid they'd think?

PROMPT 66:
What dreams have you abandoned because you decided you weren't capable or worthy?

PROMPT 67:
Who would you be if you weren't afraid of outshining others or making them uncomfortable with your success?

PROMPT 68:
Write a permission slip to yourself: What do you give yourself permission to be, do, or become?

PROMPT 69:
What would it mean to take up space unapologetically? To be seen? To be powerful?

REFLECTION: Marianne Williamson wrote, "Your playing small does not serve the world." The golden shadow is perhaps the most tragic; we bury our gifts to make others comfortable, or because we don't believe we deserve to shine.

10.5 Working with the Golden Shadow

Reclaiming your gold requires as much courage as facing your darkness, sometimes more. You must challenge the deeply held belief that you're ordinary, that your gifts belong to others, that your potential is impossible. This means:

- Recognizing projections of admiration as mirrors of your own potential
- Acknowledging your strengths without false modesty
- Allowing yourself to be seen in your fullness
- Risking others' envy or discomfort when you shine
- Believing you deserve to express your gifts

10.6 Reflection Questions:

- Who do I admire or idealize? What specific qualities do they have that I project onto them?
- What talents, gifts, or capacities have I denied or minimized in myself?
- When was I punished, shamed, or abandoned for being "too much", too smart, beautiful, powerful, creative?
- What would I do if I fully owned my capabilities and potential?

- What am I afraid would happen if I stopped playing small?
- How do I diminish myself to protect others' egos or maintain belonging?
- If someone described me the way I describe people I admire, how would I feel?

10.7 The Path Forward

Integration means withdrawing your projections of excellence and claiming your gold. This doesn't mean becoming narcissistic or arrogant, it means accurate self-perception. True humility isn't self-diminishment; it's honest awareness of both your limitations and your gifts.

You have a responsibility to your potential. Your unlived life, your unexpressed gifts, your unclaimed power, these aren't just losses for you; they're losses for the world. Whatever you came here to offer, to create, to become requires you to step into your Golden Shadow and say: "Yes, this is also mine."

Remember: Your light is not dangerous, it's necessary. The world doesn't need you smaller; it needs you whole. Every quality you've projected onto others' lives within you too, waiting to be claimed and expressed. You are not the exception to human potential, you are human, which means you contain both shadow and gold. Wholeness requires embracing both. You are allowed to be magnificent.

As you move through this chapter, practice seeing yourself through the eyes of those who love you. What do they see that you refuse to acknowledge? Your journey to the Self includes stepping into your power, owning your gifts, and finally allowing yourself to shine. This is not ego, this is integration. Claim your gold.

11
DEATH, GRIEF, AND THE THINGS WE DON'T SAY

The Shadow of Mortality

We live in a death-denying culture, and so death, along with grief, loss, and impermanence, becomes shadow material. Yet confronting mortality is essential to living authentically.

11.1 What is the Shadow of Death?

Death is the ultimate Shadow, the one certainty that modern culture works desperately to deny, avoid, and push from consciousness. Your mortality is the most fundamental truth of your existence, yet most people live as if they have infinite time, as if death happens only to others, as if this life will go on forever. In Jungian psychology, confronting death is essential to individuation and wholeness. Only by acknowledging your finitude can you live authentically and prioritize what truly matters.

Death lives in your Shadow not only as literal mortality but as all the "deaths" that comprise life: loss, endings, change, the death of identity, the death of dreams, the death of youth. To reject death is to reject half of life's cycle, birth and death, growth and decay, beginning and ending. You cannot become whole while denying the very condition that gives life its meaning.

11.2 Why Death Matters on Your Journey

Everything you've explored in this journal connects to your relationship with death. Your persona (Chapter 1) is often constructed to create an illusion of permanence and control. Your projections (Chapter 2) include projecting death onto others, believing it's something that happens "out there." Your shame (Chapter 3), anger (Chapter 4), desires (Chapter 5), and envy (Chapter 6) all intensify when you avoid facing your finitude. The victim and tyrant (Chapter 7) are both responses to the powerlessness death represents. The Unloved Child (Chapter 8) fears abandonment partly because it unconsciously knows everything ends.

And your Golden Shadow (Chapter 10)? It remains unclaimed partly because acknowledging your gifts means acknowledging you have limited time to express them. To fully live, you must first face death.

11.3 Signs You're Avoiding Death

- You live as if you have infinite time for what matters
- You distract yourself constantly from existential questions
- You panic at signs of aging or physical decline
- You avoid endings, staying in dead relationships, jobs, or identities
- You accumulate possessions or achievements to create an illusion of permanence
- You're terrified of loss and cling desperately to people and circumstances
- You've never seriously contemplated your own mortality
- You postpone meaningful action, believing "someday" will come
- You feel existentially anxious but can't name what you're afraid of

11.4 The Origins of Death Denial

Modern culture teaches death avoidance through:

- Medical advances: Creating illusion of death as optional, solvable problem
- Youth worship: Denying aging, decay, and natural cycles
- Consumer culture: Promising permanence through possessions and achievement
- Religious confusion: Either literalizing afterlife or rejecting transcendence entirely
- Disconnection from nature: Where death and rebirth are visible cycles
- Trauma avoidance: Cultural inability to be with grief, loss, and endings
- Existential terror: The raw fear of non-existence and meaninglessness

You learned to live as if death is optional, distant, or only theoretical, even though you know intellectually it's inevitable.

PROMPT 70:
What losses have you not fully grieved? Who or what have you lost that you still carry in silence?

PROMPT 71:
What are you afraid to say to the people you love because you're avoiding the reality that time is limited?

PROMPT 72:
If you knew you had one year to live, what would you change? What would suddenly matter? What would stop mattering?

PROMPT 73:
What parts of your life or your old self do you need to let die? What are you clinging to that's no longer alive?

PROMPT 74:
Write your own eulogy. What do you want your life to have meant? What do you want to be remembered for?

PROMPT 75:
How does avoiding death keep you from living fully? What risks would you take if you truly accepted your mortality?

REFLECTION: Memento mori, remember you will die. This isn't morbid; it's liberating. When we accept death, we stop postponing life. We stop waiting for permission. We become urgent about what matters.

11.5 Working with Death and Mortality

Facing death doesn't mean becoming morbid or hopeless, it means becoming real. When you acknowledge your mortality:

- You clarify what actually matters versus what you've been wasting time on
- You prioritize love, meaning, and authentic expression
- You release what's already dead, relationships, dreams, identities that no longer serve
- You value time as the precious, finite resource it is
- You stop postponing your real life
- You find freedom in accepting what cannot be controlled

Memento mori, remember you will die. This isn't depressing; it's liberating. It cuts through trivial concerns and reveals what's essential.

11.6 Reflection Questions:

- What would I do differently if I truly believed I could die at any time?
- What am I postponing until "someday?" What if someday never comes?
- What needs to die in my life, relationships, identities, dreams, that I'm keeping artificially alive?
- How does avoiding death keep me from living fully?
- What do I most fear about my own mortality?
- If I had one year left, what would I prioritize?
- What legacy do I want to leave? What mark do I want to make while I'm here?

11.7 The Path Forward

Integration means developing what Buddhists call "death awareness" and what Jung saw as necessary for wholeness, a conscious relationship with mortality that informs how you live. This includes:

- Accepting that everything ends, including you
- Grieving losses as they occur rather than accumulating unprocessed grief
- Letting die what needs to die without desperate clinging
- Living with urgency but without panic
- Making meaning in the face of finitude
- Choosing what matters when time is limited

Death gives life meaning. Without endings, nothing would matter. Your mortality is not a curse, it's what makes this moment precious, what makes your choices significant, what makes love and beauty and truth worth pursuing.

Remember: You are going to die. Everyone you love will die. Everything you build will eventually crumble. This is not nihilistic, it's reality. And within this reality lies profound freedom: you get to decide what matters in the brief, brilliant time you have.

12
INTEGRATION AND WHOLENESS

The Sacred Witness

Shadow work is not about fixing yourself. It's about seeing yourself completely, the light and the dark, the beautiful and the ugly, the acceptable and the forbidden, and embracing it all.

12.1 What is Integration?

Integration is the process of bringing together all the fragmented, rejected, and disowned parts of yourself into a unified whole. Wholeness is not perfection, purity, or the elimination of darkness, it's the acceptance and conscious relationship with all of who you are. In Jungian psychology, this is the goal of individuation: becoming the Self, the totality of your being, rather than remaining identified with the narrow ego or persona.

You've journeyed through the shadows: your persona's mask, your projections, your shame and wounds, your forbidden emotions and desires, your victim and tyrant patterns, your unloved child, your gendered shadows, your disowned gold, and your mortality. Integration means these are no longer strangers or enemies, they're recognized parts of you, each with something to offer.

12.2 Why Integration is the Ultimate Goal

Jung believed that wholeness, not perfection, is the purpose of human psychological and spiritual development. You spent the first half of life building an ego, establishing identity, fitting into society. The second half, if you're courageous, is about dissolving rigid identifications and becoming more fully yourself.

12.3 What Integration doesn't mean

- Eliminating your shadow
- Becoming perfectly balanced or peaceful
- Never struggling or feeling pain
- Transcending your humanity

12.4 What Integration means

- Consciously relating to all parts of yourself
- Making choices from awareness rather than unconscious compulsion
- Holding paradox and complexity without collapsing
- Living authentically rather than performing an acceptable image
- Allowing your full humanity, light and dark, strength and vulnerability

12.5 Signs You're Moving Toward Integration

- You can acknowledge your flaws without shame or defensiveness
- You recognize your patterns without being controlled by them
- You feel more authentic, even when it's uncomfortable
- You can hold opposing truths simultaneously (paradox)
- You project less; you see others more clearly as they are
- You claim both your wounds and your gifts
- You take responsibility for your life without victim mentality
- You set boundaries while remaining compassionate
- You're less reactive; you can pause and choose responses
- You feel both more humble and more empowered

12.6 The Ongoing Nature of Integration

Integration is not a destination you reach and then maintain forever. It's a lifelong process of:

- Noticing: Becoming aware when you're caught in old patterns
- Acknowledging: Owning what you see without judgment
- Understanding: Exploring the origins and purpose of each pattern
- Choosing: Deciding consciously how to respond rather than reacting automatically
- Allowing: Letting all parts of yourself exist without needing to eliminate them

You'll revisit the same shadows at different levels throughout your life. Each time, you have the opportunity to integrate more deeply, to relate more consciously, to choose more freely.

PROMPT 76:
Looking back at your responses in this journal, what patterns do you notice? What themes keep appearing?

PROMPT 77:
Which prompts were hardest to answer? What does that resistance tell you?

PROMPT 78:
What parts of your shadow have you begun to integrate? How do you feel different than when you started?

PROMPT 79:
What parts of your shadow still feel too difficult to face? Can you hold compassion for your resistance?

PROMPT 80:
Write a letter of gratitude to your shadow. What has it been trying to protect you from? What gifts has it been holding for you?

PROMPT 81:
How will you continue this work? What practices will help you stay conscious of your shadow moving forward?

PROMPT 82:
What does wholeness mean to you now? How is it different from perfection?

PROMPT 83:
Who are you becoming as you integrate these disowned parts? Describe this more whole version of yourself.

REFLECTION: Integration is not a destination but a practice. The shadow will continue to surprise you with new material throughout your life. Each time, return to curiosity, honesty, and compassion.

12.7 Working with Integration

The work of integration never ends, but it does get easier. As you develop a relationship with your whole self, shadow and light, you become less fragmented, less driven by unconscious forces, more available to the present moment.

12.8 Reflection Questions:

- Which parts of myself have I reclaimed through this journey?
- Where do I still feel fragmented, split, or at war with myself?
- What patterns still hook me, even though I now recognize them?
- How has my relationship with myself changed through this work?
- What does wholeness feel like in my body, my relationships, my life?
- Where am I still performing rather than being authentic?
- What would it mean to accept myself completely, shadow, wounds, gold, and all?

12.9 Living as the Self

The Self in Jungian psychology is not the ego, it's the totality of who you are, including consciousness and unconsciousness, shadow and light, personal and collective. Living as the Self means:

- No longer identifying exclusively with your persona
- Recognizing you're larger than any single role or identity
- Accepting your humanity with all its contradictions
- Living from your center rather than from others' expectations
- Making meaning even in suffering
- Contributing your unique gifts to the collective
- Accepting your place in the larger whole while honoring your individuality

This is not grandiosity, it's accurate self-perception. You are simultaneously insignificant (one small life in an infinite universe) and profoundly significant (a unique expression of consciousness that will never occur again).

12.10 The Path Forward

You've completed this journey through the shadows, but the work continues in your daily life. Integration happens not on the pages of a journal but in:

- The moment you catch yourself projecting and withdraw it
- The conversation where you set a boundary you would have avoided

- The day you choose authenticity over approval
- The time you acknowledge your gift instead of deflecting
- The relationship where you show your whole self, vulnerability included
- The ending you allow instead of clinging
- The choice made from awareness rather than fear

Remember: Wholeness is your birthright. You don't become whole through this work, you already are whole. You simply remove the barriers, the denials, the fragmentations that obscured your essential completeness. The Self you've been seeking has been here all along, waiting beneath the masks and projections and wounds.

You are not broken. You never were. You are human, complex, contradictory, containing multitudes. This is not a problem to solve but a truth to embody. Welcome home to yourself, all of yourself. This is integration. This is wholeness. This is the journey of becoming who you've always been.

You've walked through the shadows and reclaimed what was lost in the darkness. You've faced your wounds and your gold. You've acknowledged your mortality and your magnificence. Now comes the real work: living from this awareness, choosing consciousness over unconsciousness, being whole in a world that prefers you fragmented. You have everything you need. You always did. The Self awaits your recognition.

CLOSING: THE GIFT OF SHADOW WORK

You've journeyed into the depths and returned. This is the hero's journey in its most intimate form, not slaying dragons in the outer world, but meeting the dragons within and learning they were guardians all along.

The shadow is not your enemy. It never was. It's the exiled part of you that's been waiting in the dark, hoping to be brought home. Every quality you've rejected, every feeling you've suppressed, every desire you've denied, they all contain vital energy, wisdom, and power.

Wholeness is not purity. Wholeness is the integration of all that you are.

As Jung wrote: "One does not become enlightened by imagining figures of light, but by making the darkness conscious."

You have made the darkness conscious. Now comes the most important part: living with this awareness, continuing the work, and extending the same compassion to others that you've learned to give yourself.

The shadow work never ends, but it becomes easier. You've built the muscles of self-honesty and self-compassion. You've learned that you can survive seeing the truth of who you are.

And here's the paradox: the more you accept your shadow, the less power it has over you. The more you embrace your darkness, the brighter your light can shine.

Welcome home to yourself. All of you.

"Until you make the unconscious conscious, it will direct your life and you will call it fate."
*Carl Jung

ABOUT THIS JOURNAL

This journal is not a book to be read passively. It is a vessel for transformation, a mirror to hold up to the parts of yourself you've spent a lifetime avoiding. It is designed as a companion for the most important journey you will ever take, the journey inward, toward wholeness.

What This Journal Offers:

Drawing from Carl Jung's foundational concepts of the Shadow, persona, projection, and individuation, this journal provides structured prompts and reflective exercises that guide you through twelve archetypal themes. Each chapter builds upon the last, creating a progressive descent into the unconscious and an eventual return with newfound integration.

Unlike traditional self-help books that promise quick fixes or positive thinking, this journal acknowledges that true healing requires confronting what has been denied, exiled, and rejected. It honors the darkness as much as the light, recognizing that both are essential to psychological wholeness.

How to Use This Journal:

This is not meant to be completed in a single sitting, nor should it be rushed. Shadow work is deep, sometimes uncomfortable work that requires courage, honesty, and time. Some prompts may take weeks to answer fully. Others may call you back months or even years later to explore at a deeper level.

You are invited to:

- Write without censorship or judgment
- Return to difficult prompts when you're ready
- Use the margins for additional thoughts, drawings, or symbols that emerge
- Notice patterns, resistances, and revelations as they arise
- Hold yourself with compassion throughout this process
- Seek professional support if material becomes overwhelming

Who This Journal Is For:

This journal is for anyone ready to move beyond the surface of self-improvement into the depths of self-knowledge. It is for those who sense that something essential has been lost or hidden, who feel fragmented or inauthentic, who are tired of performing an acceptable version of themselves while their true self remains in exile.

It is for seekers, healers, artists, therapists, and anyone called to the ancient work of "know thyself." It is for those in midlife crisis or spiritual emergence, for those recovering from trauma or simply feeling stuck in patterns they can't break.

Most importantly, this journal is for anyone brave enough to ask: *Who am I beneath the masks I wear? What have I rejected that now controls me from the shadows? What gold have I buried that waits to be reclaimed?*

A Note on Safety:

Shadow work can bring up intense emotions, memories, and psychological material. While this journal is designed to be used independently, it is not a replacement for therapy or professional mental health support. If you have experienced significant trauma, are currently in crisis, or find yourself overwhelmed by what emerges, please reach out to a qualified therapist, particularly one trained in depth psychology or Jungian analysis.

You are not meant to do this work in complete isolation. The individuated self emerges not in solitude alone, but through conscious relationship, with oneself, with trusted others, and with the larger mysteries that hold us all.

The Promise:

If you engage this work with honesty and courage, you will not emerge unchanged. You may not feel "better" in the conventional sense, shadow work is not about feeling good; it's about feeling real. But you will become more whole, more authentic, more alive. You will reclaim energy and vitality that has been locked in maintaining false selves. You will see yourself and others with more clarity and compassion.

Most profoundly, you will discover that you are not broken and never were. You are human, complete with contradictions, complexities, and depths that far exceed the narrow persona you've been performing. This journal is your invitation to come home to the totality of who you are.

"The shadow is not a problem to be solved, but a truth to be integrated."

Welcome to the work. Welcome home.

ABOUT THE AUTHOR

Flavio Pires Molina's professional journey in healing began in dentistry, graduating from UNITAU, Brazil, in 1999. His initial interest in restoration led him to specialize in Prosthodontics at FOSJC-UNESP (2004-2006). Driven to understand the biological foundations of his work, he pursued a Master of Science in Oral Biopathology at FOSJC-UNESP (2007-2009), followed by a Ph.D. in Microbiology and Immunology at FOSJC-UNESP (2009-2011), conducting specific research on the interplay between dental implants and endotoxins.

Following his doctoral studies, during which he also served as a Lieutenant Dentist in the Brazilian Air Force (2010-2016), he moved to Europe, first to Portugal for a *Mestrado Integrado* at the University Fernando Pessoa (2016-2017). In 2017, he settled in Dublin, Ireland. He continued his advanced clinical training with a Master in Prosthodontics and New Technologies from the University of Siena, Italy (2019-2021).

To synthesize his extensive experience in science, clinical practice, and military service with a deeper understanding of the psyche, he is currently completing an MA in Jung and Post-Jungian Studies at the University of Essex. Dr. Molina's unique path allows him to approach the concept of healing with the precision of a scientist, the skill of a surgeon, and the growing perspective of a depth psychologist.

"The privilege of a lifetime is to become who you truly are."
***C.G. Jung**

BIBLIOGRAPHY AND RECOMMENDED READING

Works Referenced

Jung, Carl Gustav. *Collected Works.* Princeton University Press.

- Primary source for concepts of the Shadow, persona, projection, individuation, anima/animus, and the Self that form the theoretical foundation of this journal.

Williamson, Marianne. *A Return to Love: Reflections on the Principles of A Course in Miracles.* HarperCollins, 1992.

- Source of the quote: "Your playing small does not serve the world."

Recommended Reading for Further Shadow Work

For readers wishing to deepen their understanding and practice of shadow work, the following books offer valuable perspectives and practical guidance:

Johnson, Robert A. *Owning Your Own Shadow: Understanding the Dark Side of the Psyche.* HarperOne, 1991.

- The most accessible introduction to shadow work. Short, clear, and immediately applicable to daily life.

Zweig, Connie, and Steve Wolf. *Romancing the Shadow: A Guide to Soul Work for a Vital, Authentic Life.* Ballantine Books, 1997.

- Comprehensive guide to shadow work with practical exercises covering personal, relational, and cultural shadows.

Hollis, James. *The Middle Passage: From Misery to Meaning in Midlife.* Inner City Books, 1993.

- Essential reading on individuation in the second half of life and confronting the unlived life within.

Bradshaw, John. *Homecoming: Reclaiming and Healing Your Inner Child.* Bantam, 1990.

- Foundational work on inner child healing, shame, and reclaiming disowned parts of self.

Brown, Brené. *The Gifts of Imperfection: Let Go of Who You Think You're Supposed to Be and Embrace Who You Are.* Hazelden, 2010.

- Research-based approach to shame resilience, vulnerability, and wholehearted living.

Ford, Debbie. *The Dark Side of the Light Chasers: Reclaiming Your Power, Creativity, Brilliance, and Dreams.* Riverhead Books, 1998.

- Practical shadow work exercises focused on reclaiming both dark and golden shadow qualities.

Moore, Thomas. *Care of the Soul: A Guide for Cultivating Depth and Sacredness in Everyday Life.* HarperCollins, 1992.

- A soulful approach to living with psychological depth, honoring rather than eliminating shadow material.

Jung, Carl Gustav. *Man and His Symbols.* Dell Publishing, 1964.

- Jung's most accessible work, written specifically for general readers. An excellent starting point for understanding Jungian psychology.

www.ingramcontent.com/pod-product-compliance
Lightning Source LLC
LaVergne TN
LVHW090330210926
848480LV00004B/1365